DIGITAL AND INFORMATION LITERACY ™

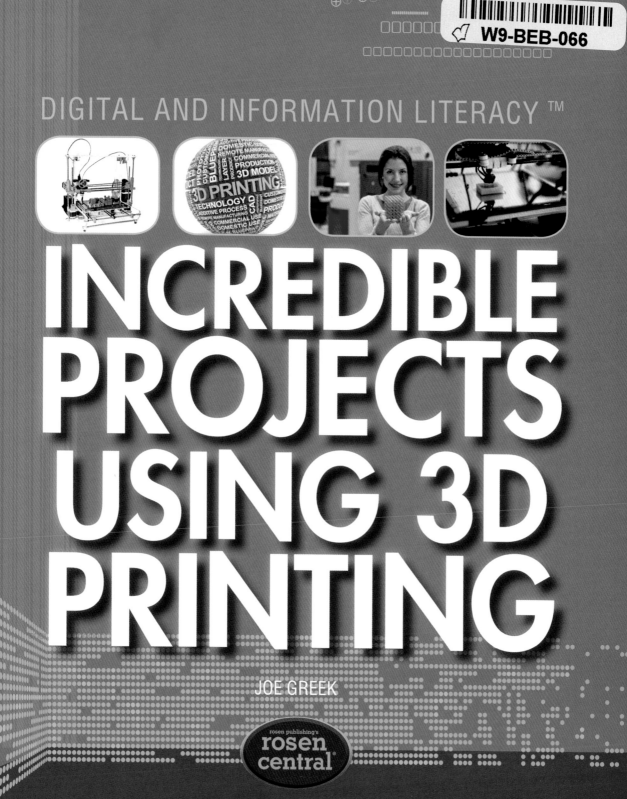

INCREDIBLE PROJECTS USING 3D PRINTING

JOE GREEK

rosen publishing's
rosen central

New York

Published in 2015 by The Rosen Publishing Group, Inc.
29 East 21st Street, New York, NY 10010

Library of Congress Cataloging-in-Publication Data

Greek, Joe, author.
Incredible projects using 3D printing/Joe Greek.—First edition.
    pages cm.—(Digital and Information literacy)
Includes bibliographical references and index.
ISBN 978-1-4777-7946-0 (library bound)—ISBN 978-1-4777-7947-7 (pbk.)—
ISBN 978-1-4777-7948-4 (6-pack)
1. Three-dimensional printing—Juvenile literature. 2. Manufacturing processes—Juvenile literature. I. Title. II. Title: Incredible projects using three-dimensional printing. III. Series: Digital and information literacy.
TS171.8.G744 2015
681.62—dc23

                                                                                    2014016052

Manufactured in Malaysia

CONTENTS

INTRODUCTION

During his 2013 State of the Union address, President Barack Obama discussed a number of topics that ranged from increasing the minimum wage to reforming immigration laws. Obama also made mention of the National Additive Manufacturing Innovation Institute (NAMII) in Youngstown, Ohio, saying: "A once-shuttered warehouse is now a state-of-the art lab where new workers are mastering the 3D printing that has the potential to revolutionize the way we make almost everything."

NAMII is a partnership between the government and numerous businesses and universities across the United States. The primary goal of NAMII is to research 3D printing, which is also known as additive manufacturing. Many people believe that the additive manufacturing production method will revolutionize manufacturing. The technology behind 3D printing has the potential to create many benefits for different industries. Supporters of the technology think that it could jump-start a new industrial revolution, reduce pollution, and create more jobs in local communities.

Traditionally, manufacturing involves techniques such as milling, sawing, machining, and turning. Referred to as *subtractive* manufacturing, these methods usually break a larger object, such as a block of metal, down into a final product by chipping, cutting, and grinding away unneeded material.

Three-dimensional printing can be used for many different projects. Here, a university lab manager in Switzerland prints a sculpture that he designed on a laptop.

However, the material that is discarded through the subtractive method can find its way into the environment to cause pollution or other harm. Additionally, from a business standpoint, the wasted materials can have a negative impact on profits.

On the other hand, *additive* manufacturing gets its name because objects are created by adding layer after layer, rather than removing material to reveal the final product within. A 3D printer can work with a variety of materials that are used in traditional manufacturing, including different types of plastics and metals, chocolate, and glass. Because 3D printing is additive, materials can be used more efficiently with less waste.

As the technology for additive manufacturing has gotten better and cheaper, it has attracted the interest of hobbyists and enthusiasts, too. Today, some creative individuals are purchasing 3D printers for their own personal use. In fact, 3D printing has become one of the cornerstones of the maker movement. The maker movement refers to the community of inventors, designers, and other innovative people who use the latest technology to make cool, one-of-a-kind, do-it-yourself (DIY) products.

Several years ago, most people had probably never even heard of 3D printing. Today, however, breakthroughs in this technology are being touted on television and the Internet on a daily basis. Are you interested in finding out more about additive manufacturing and why it could change the world? In the following sections, you will learn about this innovative technology and how it could make us rethink the way we create just about everything.

Chapter 1

Not Your Typical Printer

Television and the Internet have been abuzz about 3D printing in the past few years. To most people, it might be shocking to find out that this semi-futuristic-sounding technology has actually been around for a few decades. However, 3D printers have only found their way into people's homes recently. Now both hobbyists and professionals are pushing the boundaries of what these devices can produce. In the following sections, you will learn about 3D printing's benefits and drawbacks, the different printing methods used today, and how solid objects can be literally printed before your eyes.

What Is 3D Printing?

In 1986, Charles Hull, cofounder of 3D Systems, Inc., patented the first technique and device for printing 3D objects. The method, which is called stereolithography, turns liquid plastic into a solid by shooting it with an ultraviolet (UV) laser. Hull's machine is known as a stereolithography apparatus (SLA). By reading a computer-aided design (CAD) file, the SLA can precisely aim a UV laser at a layer of liquid plastic that turns into a solid upon contact.

Once the first layer of solid plastic has been created, the platform that it rests upon is lowered farther down into the container of liquid. Then, the UV laser shoots at the next layer of liquid until it has melded into the previous one. Layer by layer, the process is used to create prototypes that are used by many types of businesses.

Since Hull first devised stereolithography in the 1980s, different methods for producing 3D objects have been devised. Additionally, the technology and machinery used in 3D printing has changed. Prior to the past decade, 3D printers were primarily used by companies that specialized in building prototypes. Today, businesses and hobbyists are finding new uses beyond prototyping.

Many industries are exploring ways to use 3D printing in the workplace. As the technology improves, the demand for skilled workers will increase.

Researchers at many businesses are now exploring ways to benefit from 3D printing technology. They include clothing, medical, and even automobile companies. However, 3D printing still has drawbacks when compared to traditional manufacturing. For one, the ability to use 3D printing for mass production is currently limited because of the time it takes to print an object. Secondly, most manufacturing workers are still accustomed to traditional methods and are not yet trained in 3D printing. Finally, a 3D-printed object may not be as strong as one made by subtractive manufacturing.

"In 3D printing, you are building it in layers—this means that it has laminate weaknesses as the layers don't bond as well in the Z axis as they do in the X and Y plane," says Nick Allen, founder of 3D Print UK, in a 2013 Gizmodo.com article. "This is comparable to a Lego wall—you place all the bricks on top of each other, and press down: feels strong, but push the wall from the side and it breaks really easily."

3D Printing Methods

Printing a 3D object can be achieved using a number of different methods. In most cases, the printing method will depend on what type of material is being used. The following are a few of the most popular methods being used today:

- **Direct Light Processing (DLP).** Similar to stereolithography, DLP uses a projector to cast light into a vat of photopolymer—a light reactive plastic. When a layer of photopolymer has solidified, a platform lowers deeper into the vat, and the layer building process begins again.

- **Polyjet Matrix.** This method is comparable to the way that a home-office printer functions. Light reactive plastics and other materials are layered on a flat space through small nozzles that work similarly to the way an inkjet-style printer puts ink on paper. Once a layer of material has been put down, a UV light solidifies it, and then the process starts again.

File   Edit   View   Favorites   Tools   Help

GOT AN IDEA? HAVE IT PRINTED!

Got an Idea? Have It Printed!

Surging in popularity in recent years, online 3D printing businesses provide customers with the opportunity to print their own designs. Using a service, such as Sculpteo or i.materialise, you can upload a CAD file and have it printed and delivered to your home in days. Many of these types of businesses can print designs from a variety of materials. In addition to printing your design, services like Shapeways will even sell and market your custom product online and give you a percentage of the money they make.

There are several ways you can turn your idea for a 3D printable object into reality. While commercial programs are expensive and probably difficult for beginners, there are simpler programs available that can be just as productive. Google SketchUp and Autodesk 123D, for example, are free CAD programs that you can use to learn the ropes of 3D design. Also, several 3D printing services offer their own easy-to-use design programs.

- **Fused Deposition Modeling (FDM).** This method uses semi-liquids such as thermoplastics. These are solid materials that turn into a liquid above a certain temperature and back to a solid when the temperature is lowered. An FDM printer dispenses the liquid form of a thermoplastic through a heated nozzle onto a platform. Once on the platform, the layer solidifies as the temperature decreases. Some FDM printers have more than one nozzle, allowing them to print objects out of multiple materials. FDM printers can work with a variety of semi-liquids, including cheese, chocolate, and even concrete.

- **Binder Jetting.** After creating a layer from a powdered form of a material, which is generally a plastic, the printer then applies a layer of

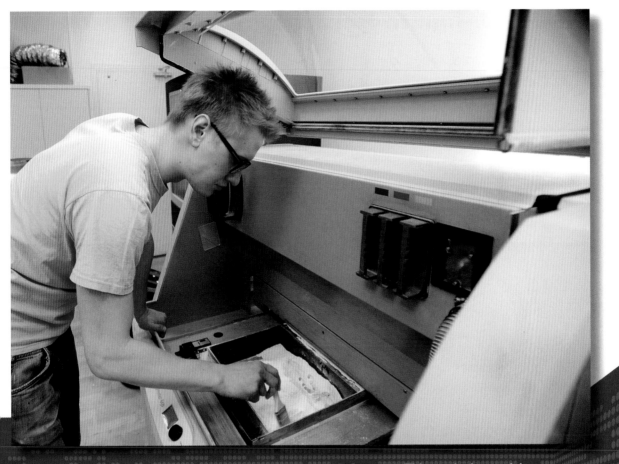

This 3D printer operator is using a ZPrinter made by 3D Systems. This particular model uses the binder jetting approach to add layer upon layer.

glue or other binding substance on top and repeats the process. Metal powders, such as bronze or stainless steel, can be printed in the same fashion. However, this requires additional time in an oven to further harden the object.

- **Selective Laser Sintering (SLS).** Like binder jetting, SLS is used primarily for working with powdered materials. However, instead of using glue between layers, SLS uses a laser to fuse—or melt—the layers together.

From Design to Finished Product

There are several ways to print 3D objects, and each technique and printer will work differently. One thing, however, that all 3D printing projects have in common is that they begin with a design. A computer functions as the brain for a 3-D printer, telling it what to do and where to place things. The CAD file acts as the instruction book that the computer uses to direct the printer.

Using a CAD program, such as 3ds Max, Maya, AutoCAD, or Photoshop CC, a designer creates a 3D model of the object he or she wishes to print. While designing a 3D printing project, a professional or

CAD programs have generally been used by engineers, architects, and trained workers. Increasingly simplified programs, such as Google SketchUp, however, are gaining more public interest.

commercial designer has to keep quality issues in mind. For example, a designer who is tasked with creating with a custom-designed bicycle frame for a client will need to consider how thick the layers should be and what type of material will be used. Understanding how the rider's weight and constant motion will affect the material and design will result in a longer-lasting bike. When creating novelty products, such as Eiffel Tower key chains, the designer won't usually have to pay as much attention to those sorts of details.

A 3D printer's nozzles are able to create objects with precision—layer by layer—by moving to locations within the CAD file that are called three-dimensional Cartesian coordinates. These coordinates, which are designated as X (left to right), Y (front to back), and Z (up and down), guide the nozzle to the different points that make up the object. The Z coordinate, according to the 3D printing company Shapeways' website, plays an important role in determining how long it takes to print an object: "A critical component of time is how many layers does an object need. If you wanted to 3D print a wineglass, the wineglass would be much more expensive if it were standing up than if it were horizontal. Adding Z, or depth, to the model is costly."

MYTHS & FACTS

MYTH Three-dimensional printers can create objects as fast as regular printers can place ink on paper.

FACT Though the speed of 3D printing has improved, the process is generally slow due to the fact that each layer has to bind with the previous one. The time this takes varies by material.

MYTH Every household should have a 3D printer.

FACT Not everybody will have the skills or desire to design custom products for his or her household. Instead, people will continue to buy parts in stores or from online vendors.

MYTH Three-dimensional printing is a replacement for current mass-production technology.

FACT It will be decades, if ever, before additive technology can truly work in a mass-production environment. To print thousands of plastic trash cans a day, for example, would take significantly longer than traditional injection molding. Additionally, it would require more 3D printers to even come close to the amount of work that traditional mass-production machinery can put out.

Chapter 2

A Fad, or Here to Stay?

dditive manufacturing has been around for many years, but most people are only now beginning to hear about it. Many businesses are just beginning to explore 3D printing as a potential replacement for subtractive manufacturing. In fact, additive manufacturing still has many drawbacks and kinks that would need to be addressed before it could replace traditional manufacturing technologies and machinery in factories. Still, personal use and interest are growing. People are finding all sorts of ways to employ 3D printers in their own lives. Could a 3D printer actually become a common sight in factories and even households?

Printing the Landscape of Manufacturing

For decades, large manufacturing companies were the only businesses that could afford 3D printers. During this time, the companies that could afford them were mainly using them for producing prototypes of parts that they would later manufacture through a traditional subtractive process. However, as the cost for plastic-printing machines dropped in recent years, the

The drastic drop in 3D printer prices has sparked a huge public interest in the technology. Here, an attendee at the 2014 International Consumer Electronics Show checks out the MakerBot Replicator Mini.

technology became more mainstream and started finding its way into smaller manufacturing businesses.

Now that more businesses and innovative groups have gained access to 3D printers, people are discovering that the technology has more applications than just prototyping. Additionally, businesses are finding that 3D printing—when done right—has the potential to change the way they run their operations. Paul Doe, chief designer at Prodrive, a motorsport technology company, told *Computer Weekly* that his business had originally used

Careers in 3D Printing

If the popularity of 3D printing continues to rise, there will be an increased need for skilled 3D designers and printer technicians. People who understand the production process and the materials that are used in 3D printing will become valuable assets to the manufacturing industry. Certification courses in additive manufacturing can be taken both offline and online. However, many employers may prefer workers who have a bachelor's or even a master's degree that is related to additive manufacturing.

Large, industrial additive manufacturing companies may rely on an entire team of variously skilled staff to take a concept from prototype to completion. If you are considering pursuing a career in 3D printing, you might consider going to college to study mechanical, chemical, or industrial engineering. Additionally, studying animation and digital design would be valuable for working with designing 3D projects. The medical industry has also heavily embraced 3D technology. A degree in biomedical technology would be crucial for getting in the door of a respectable lab that specializes in the growing study of bioprinting.

3D printing for prototyping. "But our use of the machine changed quite a lot in 18 months to actually making production parts," Doe says. "We discovered the technology was good in terms of strength, when we were using technology to make parts to test on the car."

Some researchers and advocates believe that 3D printing will change the entire manufacturing industry as we know it. For one, mass production may become a thing of the past as small-scale additive manufacturing businesses grow. Jim Chalmers of the *Guardian* predicts that "3D printing will allow production on the small-scale to be as efficient as large scale production—its existence and growth will both challenge and complete traditional manufacturing."

Furthermore, 3D printing could have far-reaching effects on the manufacturing workforce. As it is now, many countries, including the United States and Canada, have watched large numbers of manufacturing jobs move overseas to nations such as China and Indonesia because of their cheaper labor costs. However, as Professor Richard A. D'Aveni of Dartmouth College suggests in the March 2013 issue of the *Harvard Business Review*, additive manufacturing could change this. Using additive manufacturing methods will make it possible for small, local companies to create goods that can be easily altered or customized without needing to replace costly machinery and production parts. As improvements in 3D printing make customization cheaper, small-scale manufacturers may be able to compete against the costs of overseas mass production. "The great transfer of wealth and jobs to the East over the past two decades may have seemed a decisive tipping point," says D'Aveni. "But this new technology will change again how the world leans."

The Hobbyist's Dream Machine

Aside from the increase in businesses that are using additive technology, hobbyists and enthusiasts are also getting in on the 3D printing craze. So why is there a sudden interest in 3D printing for personal use?

For one, patents on different additive techniques have been expiring in recent years. "Within just a few years of the patents on FDM expiring, the price of the cheapest FDM printers fell from many thousands of dollars to as little as $300," reported Christopher Mims in an article for *Quartz* (QZ. com). "This led to a massive democratization of hobbyist-level 3D printers and injected a huge amount of excitement into the nascent movement of 'Makers,' who manufacture at home on the scale of one object at a time."

Furthermore, the Internet makes it possible for people to easily share 3D design concepts, CAD files, and knowledge with each other. With free CAD programs, such as Google SketchUp, anybody who has the patience to

Hobbyists are discovering all sorts of unique ways to use 3D printers. Using facial photographs, designers can even print action figures that resemble a person.

learn can become a self-taught 3D designer. Interestingly, there are even open-source 3D printing initiatives that provide interested individuals with the design plan to print a personal 3D printer. Fab@Home and RepRap are two of the most popular of these initiatives that have built thriving online communities. At a minimum cost, hobbyists can build their own 3D printer and then print many of the pieces that are needed to construct another printer.

Hobbyists are finding a number of uses for 3D printers. And unlike a commercial designer, a hobbyist doesn't necessarily need a printer that is top of the line in order to print something useful for himself or herself. From printing replacement plastic parts for blenders to creating customized cups, the possibilities are only limited to the individual's imagination. For example, according to a *New York Times* article by Amy O'Leary, a man in Brooklyn designed and printed a plastic adapter that makes it possible for children to connect Duplo building blocks and Brio wooden toy train tracks. Though such a project may sound useless to some, it does demonstrate how 3D printer technology makes it possible for people to create customized objects for nearly anything they can think of.

The Benefits Abound

Compared to traditional manufacturing practices, additive methods offer a number of benefits. The following are several of the main advantages that 3D printing could have on commercial and personal production:

- **New Structures.** Subtractive manufacturing techniques involve taking away materials and connecting multiple pieces to create more complicated shapes and designs. With 3D printing, more intricate pieces can be formed as one piece.

- **Less Waste.** As discussed earlier, additive manufacturing results in fewer materials going to waste. With less discarded waste, there is a reduced risk of pollution. The amount of material needed when compared to subtractive manufacturing is also smaller.

Each year, wasted material from traditional additive manufacturing ends up in the environment as litter. Three-dimensional printing can help curb the amount of waste that finds its way onto city streets and into lakes and oceans.

- **On-Site Production.** With the ability to produce or customize pieces on-site by adjusting a design file, businesses can move beyond having to special-order pieces from various manufacturers to complete a project. For example, researchers at the University of Southern California have developed a giant 3-D printer that can build a concrete home within twenty-four hours. This could reduce the laborers, materials, and time needed for large projects.

- **Increased Innovation.** Within the past few years alone, the technology and uses of 3D printing have surged. Many industries, such as biomedical technology, are finding incredible applications for additive techniques. As more people get their hands on this technology, ideas and innovations will continue to grow.

Given that mainstream interest in 3D printing has only caught on in recent years, it is difficult to tell whether or not it will become a fad or the wave of the future. Nonetheless, as you will find out in the upcoming sections, enthusiasts, researchers, and professional designers are already producing incredible projects with 3D printing.

Chapter 3

Three-Dimensional Printing Marvels

Now that 3D printers are finding their way into the hands of more enthusiasts and businesspeople, consumers are starting to get a glimpse of the capabilities of this technology. Additive manufacturing is currently making its way into several areas of daily life. The current uses range from the mouthwatering to the life-altering. In the following sections, you will learn about several of the current innovations that are being achieved through 3D printing.

Printed Prosthetics

On a daily basis, people across the world suffer from accidents and injuries that can result in the loss of a limb or other body part. To accommodate these traumatic injuries, individuals can have customizable prosthetic replacements created. Unfortunately, traditionally built prosthetics have long been expensive—sometimes costing in the tens of thousands of dollars—making them almost impossible to obtain for many people. However, 3D

Because of the comparatively inexpensive cost of production and time needed, 3D printed prosthetics may eventually become an industry standard.

printers allow designers to create fully customized prosthetics at a fraction of the cost.

In war-torn countries, civilians often become innocent victims. The African country Sudan, for example, has seen countless deaths and injuries as a consequence of civil war. Many of the injuries result in the partial or full amputation of legs and arms. Mick Ebeling, founder of the nonprofit organization Not Impossible, traveled to the country after reading a story about a boy named Daniel Omar who had lost parts of both arms in a bomb explosion. Using a 3D printer, Ebeling and others created new limbs for Omar that cost around $100. "We're hopeful that other children and adults in other regions of Africa, as well as other continents around the globe, will utilise the power of this new technology for similar beginnings," Ebeling told the *Independent*.

File   Edit   View   Favorites   Tools   Help

RECONSTRUCTING THE PAST

Reconstructing the Past

Archaeologists and researchers use a variety of tools and technologies to help people study and understand the past. Now, 3D printing has even found its place in reconstructing history so that people can see it firsthand. King Tutankhamen, better known as King Tut, was an Egyptian pharaoh who ruled from approximately 1332 BCE to 1323 BCE. When his well-preserved, elaborate tomb was discovered in 1922, the pharaoh became an instant sensation around the world. On several occasions, King Tut's mummy was showcased around the world to curious crowds.

In 2010, several important artifacts from the King Tut tomb were taken on a tour of the United States. Accompanying the items was a full-scale replica of King Tut's mummy that was incredibly detailed, down to the curves and contours of his skeletal structure. To construct the replica, natural history and prehistoric model maker Gary Staab teamed up with the 3D printing company Materialise, which owns a large, stereolithography printer. Materialise used its custom-created CAD program, called Mimics Innovation Suite, and computed tomography (CT) scans of King Tut's mummy to create a 3D model. Next, Materialise used its patented 3D printer to produce a full-sized version of the mummy made out of a photosensitive plastic material.

After the King Tut replica was completed, Staab went in and added details, including color and additional texture work. The final piece, which was nearly identical to the actual King Tut, made it possible for onlookers to have an experience that a drawing or photograph could never achieve.

Designers can also produce realistic-looking prosthetic replacements for other body parts. Ears and noses are just a couple of examples of what 3D printers are capable of producing. People aren't the only ones who can benefit from printed prosthetics, either. In 2013, a duck born without a leg in Tennessee became the first web-footed recipient of a 3D-printed limb.

Finding the Perfect Fit

In February 2014, one fashion show in New York City grabbed the attention of both technology followers and fashion lovers. Featuring 3D-printed clothing made by companies such as MakerBot and Adobe, the runway highlighted how additive technology is not limited to the production of objects that are stiff and hard.

These shoes were shown off at the 2014 3D Printshow in New York City. Designers may soon turn to 3D printing as the new wave of fashion.

Shoe companies Nike and New Balance have both experimented with producing 3D-printed shoes for athletes. New Balance, for example, used sensors to collect data on track runners' feet in 2013. By studying the runners' data, New Balance was able to design custom-fit track spike plates for each runner's shoes. To create the spikes, New Balance employed the SLS method that utilizes a powdered material. Also in 2013, Nike released its own football cleats using SLS technology. The shoe is called the Vapor Laser Talon.

However, 3D-printed clothes aren't limited just to professional athletes and models. The San Francisco, California, company Continuum sells a 3D-printed bikini called N12, which gets its name from the material used in the printing process: Nylon 12. In addition to the N12 bikini, Continuum provides customers with an online tool that allows them to create customized clothing. Similar to design programs offered by other personal 3D printing businesses, Continuum's customers can manipulate the images of a number of clothing articles and adjust the sizes to fit their own bodies.

"It's silly to say that being able to create something is limited to professionals," Continuum founder Mary Huang told the *Huffington Post*. "This is a generation of people who customize avatars, where everyone has access to creativity."

Designing for the Taste Buds

Famous chefs around the world may turn their noses up at a bowl of pasta that came out of a printer, but it is possible that someday restaurants will place 3D printers next to the oven or stovetop. For now, though, designers are using chocolate- and sugar-based materials to print intricately shaped sweets.

In January 2014, the South Carolina-based company 3D Systems unveiled the ChefJet to amazed crowds at the annual International Consumer Electronics Show. To print its sweet designs, the ChefJet uses water and dry powder ingredients. Using an additive method similar to binder jetting, the printer lays down a layer of the powdered ingredient and then sprays it with

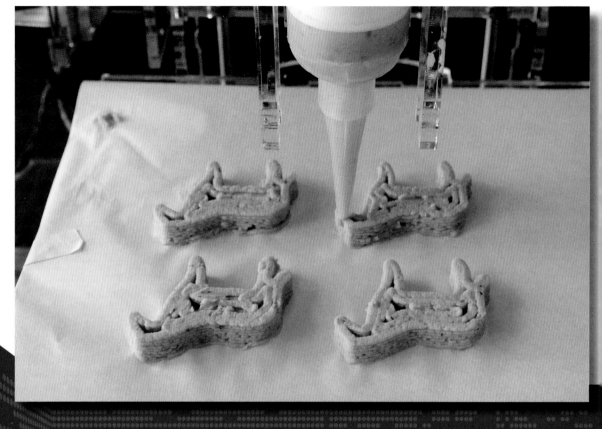

What will the kitchen of the future look like? Natural Kitchen's Foodini *(above)* is one of several 3D printers that are allowing chefs to blend technology and flavor.

water. Upon contact, the water causes the powder to crystallize—or harden—and the layering process is repeated until completed.

Beyond chocolates and candies, printers are capable of producing other kitchen classics. Natural Machines has developed a printer that is capable of printing foods that are made up of different ingredients. Using multiple containers, the Foodini can create ravioli and cookies, among other edibles. The only thing left for the chef to do is place the printed food into an oven.

Pizza, one of the world's most recognizable dishes, may one day find its way into outer space. Mechanical engineer Anjan Contractor won a $125,000 grant from NASA in 2013 to build a 3D printer that is capable of printing food for astronauts who are in space for extended periods of time. Contractor's prototype was able to successfully print a pizza. Utilizing powdered ingredients, Contractor aims to create food-printing cartridges that will have a lifespan of thirty years.

Printing a Car

Imagine that you have just received your driver's license and your parents are going to buy you a new car. So, you get online and go to a car dealership's website. There, you begin customizing your own vehicle. When you are finished, you click a button that says print. In a few days, the dealership calls to inform you that you can come by to pick up your brand-new, 3D-printed car. That is just one of many possibilities that 3D printing might be able to achieve in the future. Though technology is not quite to the point of rolling cars off a 3D-printing assembly line for the masses, many enthusiasts and organizations are making their own strides.

Kor Ecologic, an initiative of designers and engineers led by Jim Kor, have been working on an electric car that is manufactured through a mixture of additive and subtractive techniques. "With Urbee 2, more than 50 per-cent of the car will be 3D printed," Kor told Joe Bargmann of *Popular Mechanics*. "Everything you typically see and touch on the car, as you drive the car, will be 3D printed."

The engineers behind Urbee 2 use large FDM printers to produce the different parts that go into the vehicle. "The machines are so automated that the building process they perform is known as 'lights out' construction, mean-ing Kor uploads the design for a bumper, walks away, shuts off the lights and leaves," Alexander George of Wired.com wrote. "A few hundred hours later, he's got a bumper. The whole car—which is about 10 feet long—takes about 2,500 hours."

Jim Kor's Urbee has become a symbol of the innovative possibilities that 3D printing offers. Above, the Urbee is displayed at the 2013 3D Printshow exhibition in Paris.

Eventually, Kor hopes that the final version of the lightweight Urbee 2 will be capable of crossing the United States on about 10 gallons of gasoline. Though printed vehicles are not yet available to the public, the Urbee 2 may be the prototype of the next generation of vehicles.

TEN GREAT QUESTIONS

TO ASK A 3D PRINTER OPERATOR

1. What type of work do you do with 3D printing?

2. How has the technology changed since you began?

3. What kind of training is needed to get a job in 3D printing?

4. Where can a skilled 3D printer operator work?

5. What is the best additive manufacturing method?

6. What materials are easier or harder to print with?

7. Which personal 3D printer would you recommend?

8. How much would material cost for a personal 3D printer?

9. What printing projects would be good for a beginner?

10. Do you think there will be an increased need for skilled 3D printer operators?

→ Chapter 4

Printing into the Future

Technologies, such as the Internet and the telephone, changed the way we communicate—bringing people oceans apart together. Automobiles, airplanes, and ships revolutionized the way we travel. Medical breakthroughs led to longer life spans. As additive manufacturing is further explored, many different aspects of life may change for the better. In the following sections, you will learn how 3D printing could mark the beginning of a new global industrial revolution.

Bioprinting: A Medical Revolution

Perhaps one of the most beneficial and potentially world-changing innovations that may come out of additive technology is bioprinting. Researchers at universities and laboratories across the world are currently studying the use of 3D printers to produce human tissues, such as skin, bone, and even organs.

The companies Printerinks and Organovo are currently working together to print human tissue for research and rehabilitative uses, such as treating different types of skin diseases. To print human tissue, the companies are experimenting with a printing method similar to binder jetting. Using tissue

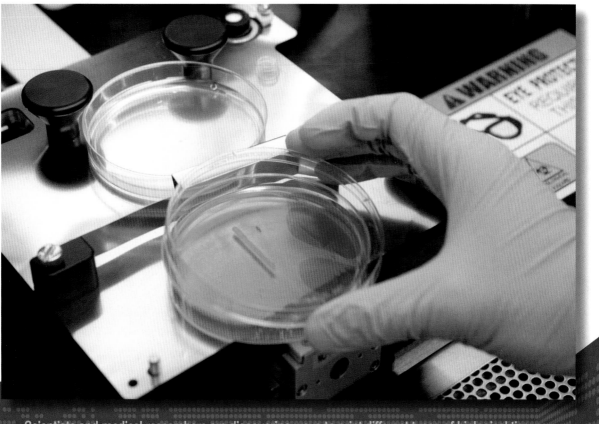

Scientists and medical researchers are discovering ways to print different types of biological tissues. The NovoGen bio printer, from Organovo, was used to print the blood vessel shown above.

samples from patients, researchers can grow new cells in a laboratory. After enough tissue cells have been produced, they are reshaped into spheres and placed into a printing cartridge. Next, a special bioprinter prints a layer of tissue cells that is followed by a layer of hydrogel, which is a supportive gelatin-like structure. Finally, researchers at Organovo remove the hydrogel and are left with human tissue that is used to test potential treatments for diseases and injuries.

Eventually, researchers hope that bioprinting may become a standard practice within the medical industry. Specifically, the technology could be used to print entire human organs, which could save countless lives. Many vital organ transplant patients die each year while waiting on a donor list. Through additive technology, doctors could take samples of a patient's tissue cells and print an organ in a matter of days. Additionally, the technology could potentially reduce the high costs that patients encounter today. However, bioprinting has also caused controversy as people have raised concerns over quality and the rights to the human tissue that the process produces.

Printing on the Battlefield

Soldiers on the battlefield may even find use for 3D printers. Currently, militaries around the world are researching and experimenting with additive manufacturing technologies. One day, soldiers could potentially carry portable 3D printers into war zones. This would allow them to print replacement parts for weaponry and other tools. Additionally, the technology could possibly be used to print drones and ammunition.

"Imagine a soldier on a firebase in the mountains of Afghanistan. A squad is attacked by insurgents. The ammunition starts to run out," Richard D'Aveni told the Associated Press. "Is it worth waiting hours and risking the lives of helicopter pilots to drop it near you, or is it worth a more expensive system that can manufacture weapons and ammunition on the spot?"

Additionally, military engineers could produce parts for vehicles and aircraft out of metals such as titanium. In fact, China is already producing 3D-printed parts for its J-15 Flying Shark jet. A 3D printer could also be used to create meals for soldiers out in the field. On a larger scale, navy lieutenants Scott Cheney-Peters and Matthew Hipple speculate that ships could be turned into giant printers capable of producing just about anything soldiers may need in the field, according to Wired.com.

Utilizing 3D printers would allow militaries to reduce their dependence on certain parts of their supply chains—trucks, planes, and ships that deliver goods. This would save money, fuel, time, and possibly lives. However, soldiers are not the only people who could use 3D printers for battle. Terrorist

The increased popularity of personal 3D printers has even created questions about the harm they could potentially pose. Above, Cody Wilson works on the first gun to be made entirely through 3D printing.

and criminal organizations may also find that additive technology can be used to their advantage. For example, CAD files to print guns have already been created and distributed online. Many governments are passing laws, however, that ban people from using 3D printers to produce weapons.

Treating War Injuries

Soldiers are often put on the front lines of danger. In countries such as Afghanistan and Iraq, thousands of men and women in the armed forces of the United States and its allies have died. In addition, many soldiers have returned to their homes with serious injuries that range from amputated limbs to severe burns that leave them barely recognizable to friends and families. According to the Armed Forces Institute of Regenerative Medicine, burn injuries make up 5 to 20 percent of the injuries soldiers suffer. Researchers at the Wake Forest Institute for Regenerative Medicine have been experimenting with bioprinting to create replacement skin for soldiers. Through funding from the U.S. Department of Defense, researchers hope to one day be able to provide treatment to soldiers and civilians alike.

Printers in Space!

NASA plans to send a 3D printer with astronauts to the International Space Station (ISS). Having a 3D printer aboard the ISS will allow astronauts to produce spare parts and tools in a zero-gravity environment. Since astronauts only have access to the items aboard the ISS, they run the risk of landing in a life-threatening situation if they don't have the necessary tools during an emergency. Such a situation occurred to members of the Apollo 13 mission in 1970 when they had to craft a carbon dioxide filter from a plastic bag and other loose items. A 2013 article by the BBC pointed out that the situation could have potentially been avoided if 3D printing technology had existed at the time. "If you want to be adaptable, you have to be able to design and manufacture on the fly, and

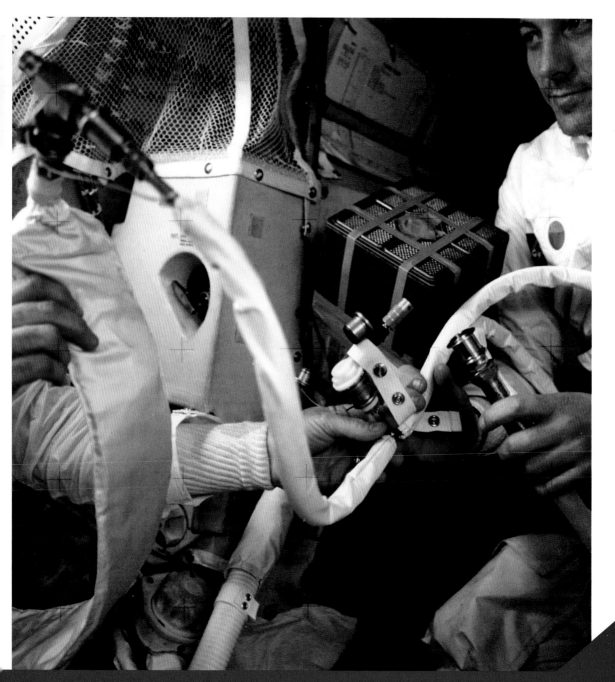

Apollo 13 astronaut John L. Swigert Jr. *(right)* holds part of the temporary system that was created from random parts amid an emergency situation miles above Earth's atmosphere.

that's where 3D printing in space comes in," Dave Korsmeyer, director of engineering at NASA's Ames Research Center, is quoted as saying in the same article.

Beyond the ISS, 3D printers could be used in long-term missions and even for colonization of the moon or neighboring planets. A 3D printer might even be able to use materials found on another planet to construct a habitat in which people could live. According to an article on Discovery.com, the European Space Agency has teamed up with an architecture firm to research the potential of using materials found in the moon's soil to print full-sized structures. Using materials on Earth that are

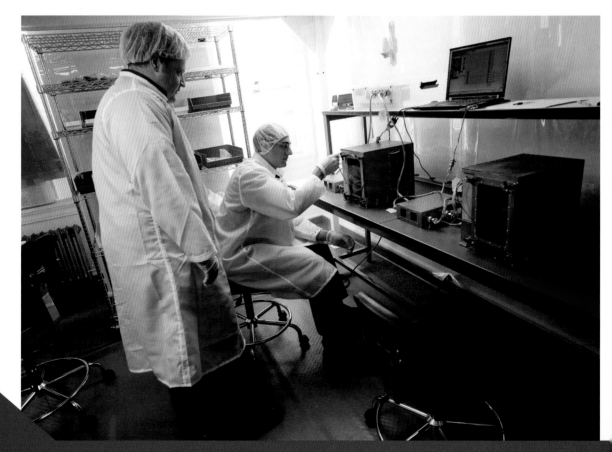

Made in Space employees Matthew Napoli *(left)* and Michael Snyder *(right)* test out a 3D printer designed for use on the International Space Station (ISS).

similar to what can be found on the moon, researchers from the United Kingdom-based company Monolite achieved positive results. "First, we needed to mix the simulated lunar material with magnesium oxide. This turns it into 'paper' we can print with," says Monolite founder Enrico Dini. "Then for our structural 'ink,' we apply a binding salt which converts material to a stone-like solid." It may be several decades before 3D printers actually create inhabitable environments outside of Earth's own atmosphere, but the first steps are already being taken.

Considering that additive manufacturing has been around for several decades, it's amazing that it has taken so long for most of its potential uses to become a reality. Whether 3D printing will become a fad that is replaced by another technology within a few years, or whether it will truly change the world is yet to be seen. For the moment, it is impossible to ignore the fact that a technology that sounds like something out of the future is unveiling its innovative potential today!

GLOSSARY

additive manufacturing The process of creating an object layer by layer; also called 3D printing.

cell A small, often microscopic structure that combines with other cells to create larger organs, such as skin.

computer-aided design (CAD) The use of a computer to create and modify a design.

drone An aircraft that does not have a pilot and is often used for surveillance.

industrial revolution The introduction of new or improved technologies or production methods to create a sudden change in an economy.

initiative An organization or partnership that is created with the intent to improve, promote, and discover new knowledge.

injection molding The process of shaping a material, such as rubber or plastic, by injecting it into a hollow container in its heated or liquid state.

innovation The discovery of a new idea, method, or product.

mass production The production of large numbers of the same object.

open source Software that is free to anyone and can be modified or redistributed.

patent A government-authorized license that makes it illegal for other people or businesses to make, use, or sell an individual's invention for a period of time.

prototype A test version or model of a final product.

replica An exact copy of something.

subtractive manufacturing Any method for creating objects that involves material being removed.

ultraviolet (UV) light A kind of light that cannot be seen by the human eye and has the power to break certain chemical bonds.

FOR MORE INFORMATION

America Makes
236 W. Boardman Street
Youngstown, OH 44503
(330) 622-4299
Website: https://www.americamakes.us
America Makes (also known as the National Additive Manufacturing
    Innovation Institute) is a U.S. government–backed program consisting of
    businesses, universities, and governmental groups that work together to
    accelerate the research, discovery, and innovation of additive
    manufacturing.

American Design Drafting Association (ADDA)
105 East Main Street
Newbern, TN 38059
(731) 627-0802
Website: http://www.adda.org
ADDA is a nonprofit organization for professionals and students who work
    with CAD in different industries.

Association for Computer Aided Design in Architecture (ACADIA)
Website: http://www.acadia.org
ACADIA is an international organization for digital design researchers and
    professionals. The group's goal is to research and improve innovation
    in design creativity, sustainability, and education.

CAD Society
(888) 537-6434
Website: http://www.cadsociety.org
The CAD Society is a nonprofit organization of professionals working with

CAD programs in various industries. The organization's goal is to establish community and open communication among members.

Canadian Society for Mechanical Engineering
1295 Highway 2 East
Kingston, ON K71 4V1
Canada
(613) 547-5989
Website: http://www.csme-scgm.ca
This organization for Canadian mechanical engineers promotes professional development through seminars, publications, and international events.

RepRap
Website: http://www.reprap.org
RepRap is an open-source, online initiative that provides free CAD files that anyone can use to print a non-patented 3D printer.

Websites

Because of the changing nature of Internet links, Rosen Publishing has developed an online list of websites related to the subject of this book. This site is updated regularly. Please use the following link to access the list:

http://www.rosenlinks.com/DIL/3DPr

FOR FURTHER READING

Anderson, Chris. *Makers: The New Industrial Revolution*. New York, NY: Crown Business, 2012.

Barnatt, Christopher. *3D Printing: The Next Industrial Revolution*. Seattle, WA: CreateSpace Independent Publishing Platform, 2013.

Budmen, Isaac, and Anthony Rotolo. *The Book on 3D Printing*. Seattle, WA: CreateSpace Independent Publishing Platform, 2013.

Diana, Carla. *LEO the Maker Prince: Journeys in 3D Printing*. Sebastopol, CA: Maker Media, Inc., 2013.

France, Anna Kaziunas. *Make: 3D Printing: The Essential Guide to 3-D Printers*. Sebastopol, CA: Maker Media, Inc., 2013.

Hausman, Kalani Kirk, and Richard Home. *3D Printing for Dummies*. Hoboken, NJ: Wiley, 2014.

Heller, Steven, and Teresa Fernandes. *Becoming a Graphic Designer: A Guide to Careers in Design*. Hoboken, NJ: Wiley, 2010.

Kemp, Adam. *The Makerspace Workbench: Tools, Technologies, and Techniques for Making*. Sebastopol, CA: Maker Media, Inc., 2013.

Lang, David. *Zero to Maker: Learn (Just Enough) to Make (Just About) Anything*. Sebastopol, CA: Maker Media, Inc., 2013.

O'Neill, Terence, and Josh Williams. *3D Printing* (21st Century Skills Innovation Library: Makers as Innovators). North Mankato, MN: Cherry Lake Publishing, 2013.

Prusa, Josef. *Getting Started with RepRap: 3D Printing on Your Desktop*. Sebastopol, CA: Maker Media, Inc., 2014.

Vaughan, William. *Digital Modeling*. Upper Saddle River, NJ: New Riders, 2012.

BIBLIOGRAPHY

Bargmann, Joe. "Urbee 2 the 3D-Printed Car That Will Drive Across the Country." *Popular Mechanics*, November 4, 2013. Retrieved February 2014 (http://www.popularmechanics.com/cars/news/industry/urbee-2-the-3d-printed-car-that-will-drive-across-the-country-16119485).

Barnatt, Christopher. "3D Printing." ExplainingTheFuture.com, November 10, 2013. Retrieved February 2014 (http://www.explainingthefuture.com/3dprinting.html).

Beckhusen, Robert. "In Tomorrow's Wars, Battles Will Be Fought with a 3-D Printer." Wired.com, May 17, 2013. Retrieved February 2014 (http://www.wired.com/dangerroom/2013/05/military-3d-printers).

Chalmers, Jim. "3D Printing: Not Yet a New Industrial Revolution, but Its Impact Will Be Huge." *Guardian*, December 10, 2013. Retrieved February 2014 (http://www.theguardian.com/commentisfree/2013/dec/11/3d-printing-not-yet-a-new-industrial-revolution-but-its-impact-will-be-huge).

D'Aveni, Richard A. "3-D Printing Will Change the World." *Harvard Business Review*, March 2013. Retrieved February 2014 (http://hbr.org/2013/03/3-d-printing-will-change-the-world).

Hall, Kathleen. "How 3D Printing Impacts Manufacturing." ComputerWeekly.com, February 2013. Retrieved February 2014 (http://www.computerweekly.com/feature/How-3-D-printing-impacts-manufacturing).

Hindman, Nate C. "Continuum's 3-D Printed Clothing Offers a Glimpse into the Future of Fashion." *Huffington Post*, May 30, 2013. Retrieved February 2014 (http://www.huffingtonpost.com/2013/04/16/continuum-3-d-printed-clothing_n_3093541.html).

Mendoza, Martha. "3-D Printing Goes from Sci-Fi Fantasy to Reality." Associated Press, June 2, 2013. Retrieved February 2014 (http://bigstory.ap.org/article/3-d-printing-goes-sci-fi-fantasy-reality).

New Balance. "New Balance Pushes the Limits of Innovation with 3D
    Printing." Press release, March 7, 2013. Retrieved February 2014
    (http://www.newbalance.com/New-Balance-Pushes-the-Limits-of
    -Innovation-with-3D-Printing/press_2013_New_Balance_Pushes
    _Limits_of_Innovation_with_3D_Printing,default,pg.html).
Stenovec, Timothy. "The ChefJet 3D Printer Prints Dessert, and Yes, It's Really
    Good." *Huffington Post*, January 10, 2014. Retrieved February 2014
    (http://www.huffingtonpost.com/2014/01/10/chefjet-3d-printer
    -food_n_4573271.html).
Vincent, James. "3D Printed Prosthetics: How a $100 Arm Is Giving Hope to
    Sudan's 50,000 War Amputees." *Independent*, January 20, 2014.
    Retrieved February 2014 (http://www.independent.co.uk/life-style/
    gadgets-and-tech/news/3dprinted-prosthetics-how-a-100-arm-is
    -giving-hope-to-sudans-50000-war-amputees-9071708.html).
Williams, Rhiannon. "The Next Step: 3D Printing the Human Body."
    Telegraph, February 11, 2014. Retrieved February 2014 (http://
    www.telegraph.co.uk/technology/news/10629531/The-next
    -step-3D-printing-the-human-body.html).

INDEX

About the Author

Joe Greek is a writer who has been obsessed with technology since elementary school. He has written for magazines, newspapers, and the Internet, covering topics that range from the stock market to web design. Additionally, he is a published author of technology-related books for students, including *Social Network-Powered Information Sharing* and *Writing Term Papers with Cool New Digital Tools*.

Photo Credits

Cover and p. 1 (from left) © iStockphoto.com/bluehill75, © iStockphoto.com/German, © iStockphoto.com/Latsalomao, © iStockphoto.com/seraficus; p. 5 Gaetan Bally/Keystone/Redux; p. 8 Monty Rakusen/Cultura/Getty Images; p. 10 © ITAR/TASS/ZUMA Press; p. 12 Ethan Miller/Getty Images; pp. 16, 35, 38 © AP Images; pp. 19, 28 Rex Features/AP Images; p. 21 Karen Huang; p. 24 Bloomberg/Getty Images; p. 26 Anadolu Agency/Getty Images; p. 30 Joel Saget/AFP/Getty Images; p. 33 © K.C. Alfred/The U-T San Diego/ZUMA Press; p. 37 NASA; cover and interior pages (dots graphic) © iStockphoto.com/suprun; interior pages (browser window graphic) © iStockphoto.com/AF-studio.

Designer: Nicole Russo; Editor: Jeanne Nagle
Photo Researcher: Karen Huang